Building Better Marriages in Oklahoma

Building Better Marriages in Oklahoma

Drs. Les & Leslie Parrott

Tulsa, Oklahoma

Unless otherwise indicated, all Scripture quotations are taken from the *Holy Bible, New International Version*®. NIV®. Copyright © 1973, 1978, 1984 by International Bible Society. Used by permission of Zondervan Publishing House. All rights reserved.

Scripture quotations marked KJV are taken from the *King James Version* of the Bible.

Building Better Marriages in Oklahoma
ISBN 1-58919-303-2
Copyright © 2001 by Les and Leslie Parrott
Center for Relationship Development
Seattle Pacific University
Seattle, Washington 98119

Published by RiverOak Publishing
P.O. Box 700143
Tulsa, Oklahoma 74170-0143

The Oklahoma Marriage Initiative recognizes and thanks the University of Central Oklahoma for usage of the artwork of the 50th anniversary of the musical *Oklahoma* featured on the book cover.

*Grateful acknowledgment is made to Bill Morelan for the use of excerpts from his book *How to Stay Married for Life,* published by Honor Books, Tulsa Oklahoma. Copyright © 1996. Used by permission of Honor Books. These excerpts are noted with an asterisk.

Printed in the United States of America. All rights reserved under International Copyright Law. Contents and/or cover may not be reproduced in whole or in part in any form without the express written consent of the Publisher.

> **Sweetheart, they're suspecting things,
> People will say we're in love.**
>
> —Rogers and Hammerstein
> *Oklahoma*

Introduction

We moved from Seattle to Oklahoma City this year. It's not a permanent move. But for twelve months we will live in this city and work with the Governor's office on one of the nation's most innovative and surprising social programs.

After Nevada, you see, Oklahoma has the highest divorce rate in the nation. Right here in what some describe as the buckle of the Bible-Belt, marriages are crumbling at alarming rates. Surprised? You're not the only one. In fact, you are in the same company as your Governor.

Speculations on why Oklahoma would have such a disturbing divorce rate are many. But Governor Frank Keating is not waiting passively for social scientists to pin-point answers. He and the First Lady are doing something radical. In an all-out, unprecedented move, the Keatings formed the first ever state-wide marriage initiative with a bold goal: To reduce the divorce rate in Oklahoma by a third in the next ten years. What's more, the Governor has devoted ten million dollars to make it happen. No governor in U.S. history has ever focused more energy—or money—on marriage.

So when we received a call inviting us to be part of such an unprecedented undertaking to build better marriages throughout an entire state, we didn't have to think twice. As the Governor's "marriage ambassadors," it is our job to raise the public level of awareness about marriage and to equip as many couples as possible for life-long love. This assignment, of course, is not without its challenges. Already, in the short time we have been here, we have discovered many sincere couples with no more preparation for marriage than a wing and prayer. Literally.

So in an effort to get Oklahomans thinking more seriously about marriage, we have compiled this little book of quotes and quips. As you thumb through it you'll find all kinds of information—from the lighter side of "where to kiss in Oklahoma" to the more insightful "best marriage advice you've ever heard." This may not be the most exhaustive or profound marriage book you've ever read, but it just may get you thinking about how you can play a part in helping the Governor and fellow Oklahomans build better marriages in Oklahoma.

Drs. Les and Leslie Parrott
Oklahoma Marriage Scholars in Residence

Foreword

What is a family?

Wonderful, nurturing families come in all shapes and sizes, but there can be little doubt that children raised in healthy, intact families have a distinct advantage. Children of divorce are far more likely to live in poverty at some time during their crucial formative years. They all too often experience school problems or stray into crime or experimentation with drugs and alcohol. There is extensive research that suggests children from fractured homes have more trouble as adults in building and sustaining healthy relationships, and may even be more likely to be involved in abuse. The social costs of divorce are extensive: so are the personal and emotional costs.

After decades of debate, the verdict is in: divorce hurts. When a family comes apart, the wounds are deep and long lasting. Government can do some things to help, but reversing this unhealthy trend is really a matter of the heart. A good place to start is with our collective attitude about divorce. We need the courage to challenge what has become conventional wisdom for too many Americans—a mistaken belief that marriage is a disposable contract.

Our Marriage Initiative is the first program of its kind in America, an effort to change the way we think about marriage and divorce. We originally launched the initiative in response to Oklahoma's high divorce rate, which placed our state, year after year, near the top (or bottom, to be more realistic) in the number of marriages that failed. With strong support from a wide spectrum of religious and community groups, this initiative has blossomed into a movement to preserve and restore Oklahoma families.

As a part of that initiative, Drs. Les and Leslie Parrott, renowned experts on the subject of marriage, have come to Oklahoma as our Marriage Ambassadors. In that role they have assembled this little book—facts about marriage, plus some wise words from a wide variety of Oklahomans. This book is designed to encourage you as an Oklahoman to make your marriage everything it was meant to be. Read it, and we think you will agree that preserving Oklahoma families is a job for all of us—and the right thing to do!

Governor Frank Keating
First Lady Cathy Keating

I can't imagine any social cause that has more far-reaching and meaningful implication for Oklahoma than marriage. While there are plenty of positive economic and societal changes that occur when marriages are stable, I'm empowered by the personal fulfillment that our citizens enjoy when their marriages are healthy and strong. After thirty-three years of marriage, it is something Sharyn and I can personally attest to.

—Jerry Regier
Secretary for Oklahoma Health
and Human Services
Oklahoma City, Oklahoma

The Oklahoma spirit is strong and unique. We have worked through so many difficult times throughout our history; surely we can find solutions to work through the problems in our marriages. The road can be challenging, but the rewards many.

*—Christopher and Meg Salyer,
married 1984*

Relationships are exhausting until we figure out how to direct our energies in ways that [the opposite gender] can truly appreciate. Then we all win.

—John Gray

It's no mistake that *maturity* and *matrimony* come from the same word.

> —*Drs. Les and Leslie Parrott*
> *Oklahoma Marriage Ambassadors*

Love is like a tennis match; you'll never win consistently until you learn to serve well.

—Dan P. Herod

Commitment looks toward a future that cannot be seen, and promises to be there.

—Drs. Les and Leslie Parrott
Oklahoma Marriage Ambassadors

Make a tradition to do something every year to strengthen your relationship.

—Dr. Don and Jennifer Hebbard,
married 1981
Edmond, Oklahoma

Marriage is not a 50/50 deal. It is a man and a woman giving 100% of themselves to each other.

—*Dr. Ted and Jerri Kersh, married 1970*
Oklahoma City, Oklahoma

There is nothing in the world worse than a bad marriage, and at the same time nothing better than a good one.

—Drs. Les and Leslie Parrott
Oklahoma Marriage Ambassadors

No marriage, no matter how good, is immune to bad things. We all start out smoothly on the road of love but we eventually stub our toe on something we didn't expect. It's how we adjust to the unexpected that makes all the difference.

—Drs. Les and Leslie Parrott
Oklahoma Marriage Ambassadors

Marital unhappiness is never caused by only one person. That's why therapists focus not on *who* is wrong, but *what* is wrong.

—Drs. Les and Leslie Parrott
Oklahoma Marriage Ambassadors

Marriage Booster

Many people fail to express their love to the very person they love the most.

Test yourself.

Do you express your love and appreciation for your spouse:

- More than once a day?
- More than once a week?
- More than once a month?

Be honest and if you find you've been missing the boat, turn over a new leaf today!

Love, by itself, is not enough to sustain even the most loving couples—at least the kind of love Hollywood pumps into our culture is not enough. Marriage requires new skills in communication, conflict resolution and so on. Love cannot protect a marriage from harm. But love combined with effective skills can overcome all.

—Drs. Les and Leslie Parrott
Oklahoma Marriage Ambassadors

A man will leave his father and mother and be united to his wife, and they will become one flesh.

GENESIS 2:24

There is no more lovely, friendly, and charming relationship, communion, or company than a good marriage.

—*Martin Luther*

God did not intend for man or woman to be alone and through marriage we are made complete in the eyes of God.

> —*Bob Ricks*
> *Commissioner for Oklahoma*
> *Department of Public Safety*
> *Oklahoma City, Oklahoma*

Every day in every marriage, choices are made that keep couples headed where they want to go or lead them to places that they dread.

—Drs. Les and Leslie Parrott
Oklahoma Marriage Ambassadors

Marriage is more than "Wilt Thou?" or an "I do!" It's a two-person pledge to a binding and supportive relationship, whose highest potential is reached through a shared allegiance to the will of God.

—Dr. Stan Toler,
Pastor, Trinity Church of the Nazarene
Author
Oklahoma City, Oklahoma

One of the best things a couple can do from time to time is review the choices they made, both good and bad, that have shaped the current state of their relationship.

—Drs. Les and Leslie Parrott
Oklahoma Marriage Ambassadors

To Maintain a . . .

Never treat your spouse like he or she is last on your priority list.

Never respond to your spouse's loving advances by laughing hysterically and snarling "Get real!"

Never extol the virtues of your former love interest and reminisce about "the good old days" before you got married.

... Happy Marriage

Always treat your spouse like he or she is #1 on your priority list.

Always, when your spouse feels amorous, look for creative new ways to express your love.

Always look for ways to remind your spouse that he or she is your favorite person in the world.

Every successful marriage requires necessary losses. For starters, marriage means coming to terms with new limits on one's independence.

—Drs. Les and Leslie Parrott
Oklahoma Marriage Ambassadors

Marriage isn't a 50/50 proposition. Marriage is a partnership that requires each partner to give more than the other at times—more understanding, more consideration, and so on. The willingness to give more than your partner is what makes a strong and lasting marriage.

—Ron Cupp
Oklahoma City, Oklahoma

Have fun just being together.

—Arthur and Mabel Johnson,
married 1920
Oklahoma City, Oklahoma

Arthur and Mabel met when he came to pick up his brother's engagement ring she was returning. "Six months later we were married," Mabel says laughing. During their seventy-three years of marriage, they took lots of little "day trips" and numerous vacations.*

When you say, "If this person needs me, I'll be complete," you are reducing others to projects on your relationship resume.

—Drs. Les and Leslie Parrott
Oklahoma Marriage Ambassadors

Most Romantic Place to Kiss in Oklahoma

The most romantic place in Oklahoma to kiss your spouse is the Gilcrease Rose Garden at dawn.

—Lyndal Whitworth, married 1962
Stillwater, Oklahoma

In Tahlequah at the headquarters of the Cherokee Nation.

—Patrick and Pamela McGuigan,
married 1976
Oklahoma City, Oklahoma

Living happily ever after only works if you make it work.

—Drs. Les and Leslie Parrott
Oklahoma Marriage Ambassadors

What are the four most intimidating words in a couple's vocabulary?

"We need to talk."

—Drs. Les and Leslie Parrott
Oklahoma Marriage Ambassadors

Learn something new about your spouse every day and give thanks for what you have learned.

—John and Sharon Yeats, married 1970
Oklahoma City, Oklahoma

Be patient, become best friends, realize that disappointments will be part of your lives but that together you can thrive.

—Bill and Michelle Donahue,
married 1973
Tulsa, Oklahoma

Love doesn't make the world go 'round.
Love is what makes the ride worthwhile.

—Franklin P. Jones

Did You Know?

The number one trait that Americans, both men and women, claim they look for first in a prospective mate is:

A sense of humor!

The number two trait?

Intelligence!

Love to faults is always blind,
    Always is to joy inclin'd,
        Lawless, wing'd, and unconfin'd,
            And breaks all chains from every mind.

—William Blake

The supreme happiness of life is the conviction that we are loved.

—Victor Hugo

Best Date Place in Oklahoma

Norman's Chocolate Festival.

> *—Rabbi David and Nina Packman,*
> *married 1960*
> *Oklahoma City, Oklahoma*

The Myriad Gardens.

> *—George and Thelma Young,*
> *married 1987*
> *Oklahoma City, Oklahoma*

Each morning, before getting out of bed, pray together.

Find fun things to do together.

Associate with other couples who work at having healthy marriages.

—Buz and Cindy Walker, married 1976
Tulsa, Oklahoma

Spirituality is to marriage what yeast is to bread. Ultimately, your spiritual commitment will determine whether your marriage rises successfully or falls disappointingly flat.

> —Drs. Les and Leslie Parrott
> *Oklahoma Marriage Ambassadors*

Enter into marriage with your eyes wide open, and then keep them half-closed thereafter! Show your unselfishness in everything you do for each other. It comes back tenfold.

>   —A.G. and Ruth Meyers, married 1954
>   Oklahoma City, Oklahoma

Romance is a fragile flower, and it cannot long survive where it is ignored or taken for granted. Without commitment and imagination, it will slowly wither and die. But for those who are committed to keeping romance in their marriage, the best is yet to come.

—*Richard Exley*

Every marriage at every stage in the relationship needs a good sloshin' of creativity. Have fun, be creative with approaches to keep your marriage fresh and alive.

—Anthony Jordan
Exec. Director/Treasurer
Baptist General Convention
of Oklahoma
Marriage Initiative Religious
Sector Leader
Oklahoma City, Oklahoma

Attitude. It can make a world of difference in how two people view the same thing, especially in marriage. And few things are more toxic to a couple than a bad attitude that pervades a good marriage.

—Drs. Les and Leslie Parrott
Oklahoma Marriage Ambassadors

Happy couples don't have a certain set of circumstances. They have a certain set of attitudes.

—Drs. Les and Leslie Parrott
Oklahoma Marriage Ambassadors

Learn to bend and not break.

—Gerald and Evelyn Smith,
  married 1946
  Oklahoma City, Oklahoma

Gerald and Evelyn met soon after he returned from World War II. Evelyn was renting a duplex from his parents, and Gerald came to fix the oven. "He just wouldn't leave, so I asked him for supper," says Evelyn. "He still wouldn't leave—so I married him!"*

The House Beautiful

The Crown of the house is godliness.
The Beauty of the house is order.
The Glory of the house is hospitality.
The Blessing of the house is contentment.
The Spirit of the house is joy.

—Anonymous

The more couples focus on what they have in common, the deeper intimacy grows.

—Drs. Les and Leslie Parrott
Oklahoma Marriage Ambassadors

Choose to stay in love—commitment is a choice, not a feeling. If you are looking for ways to meet your spouse's needs, you won't have time to notice if yours are being met—but they will be.

*—Kirk and Jan Jewell,
married 1972*

So God created man in his own image, in the image of God he created him; male and female he created them.

GENESIS 1:27

Marriage Booster!

It's a good thing to prime the pump by showing some simple gesture of kindness:

- Taking out the garbage or fixing the light switch without being asked
- Baking a favorite dessert or cleaning out the closet "just because"
- Offering to pick up the kids or to run errands for your spouse
- Gassing up the car and getting a deluxe car wash

If you look for little things to do for your spouse, you're likely to find them. And if you do those simple acts of kindness, you'll be surprised at how much they will be appreciated.

Invest in your relationship with your spouse for the long-term. And remember a commitment is something you do even when you don't feel like it.

—Jack and Linda Bowen, married 1969
Oklahoma City, Oklahoma

A happy marriage cannot survive the cancer of resentment.

Like self-pity and blame, it eats at the human spirit and kills the capacity for joy.

—Drs. Les and Leslie Parrott
Oklahoma Marriage Ambassadors

Do not talk bad about your spouse to your spouse's family.

*—Dennis and Sherry Yelton,
married 1975*

Bad things happen to good marriages when we expect our partner to think, feel and behave the way we want them to. Each unrealistic expectation is like a link in a heavy chain that increasingly binds us to a disappointing marriage.

—Drs. Les and Leslie Parrott
Oklahoma Marriage Ambassadors

What is the most dramatic loss experienced in a new marriage?

The idealized image you have of your partner.

—*Drs. Les and Leslie Parrott*
 Oklahoma Marriage Ambassadors

Questions to Ponder

In life, we often get what we want most! For example, deeper and more meaningful relationships can be achieved by setting aside the fulfillment of self-centered desires.

- What do you want most?
- Are you willing to put the goals and desires of another person before your own?

Someone asked me
To name the time
Our friendship stopped
And love began.
Oh my darling,
That's the secret.
Our friendship
Never stopped.

—Lois Wyse

The failure to give or receive forgiveness probably accounts for nearly every marriage that does not endure.

—Drs. Les and Leslie Parrott
Oklahoma Marriage Ambassadors

Did You Know?

A survey found that 75 percent of those polled were more tolerant of their pets' misdeeds than those of their spouses or children.

A wise lover values not so much the gift of the lover as the love of the giver.

—*Thomas à Kempis*

Learn to love and appreciate the good in each other.

> —*Joseph and Lenora Holland,*
> *married 1939*
> *Watts, Oklahoma*

Joseph and Lenora are "complete opposites in disposition," yet have learned to work together toward common goals. Joseph was a carpenter when they married, served in World War II as a combat engineer, and later became a pastor. "You must always love and appreciate each other," says Lenora.*

A happy marriage is the union of two good forgivers.

—Ruth Bell Graham

Learn to put up with his little quirks—he's learned to put up with yours!

> —Lloyd and Doris Mitchell,
> married 1934
> Jay, Oklahoma

Doris first saw Lloyd as he drove his parents' covered wagon past her school on the way to a new homestead. "I told the other girls, 'That tall boy's mine!'" she remembers with a laugh. "And sure enough, he was!"*

To Maintain a . . .

Never tell your wife that your mother's cooking is better than hers.

Never tell your husband that your father was a better handyman than he is.

Never criticize your spouse in public.

. . . Happy Marriage

Always show your wife appreciation—and be sure to brag on her cooking!

Always show your husband appreciation—and be sure to brag on his Mr. Fix-it projects.

Always look for ways to praise your spouse in public.

Intimacy is the mystical bond of friendship, commitment, and understanding.

—Neil Warren

Most Romantic Place to Kiss in Oklahoma

In Kenton, at the top of the Black Mesa in the panhandle because it's so beautiful and unlike any other part of the state (it may also have something to do with the altitude).

—Jack and Betty Frank, married 1989
Tulsa, Oklahoma

We're still searching for this place!

—Mike and Ann McCarville,
married 1962
Oklahoma City, Oklahoma

Never stop giving to your spouse. Forgive for your own sake, as well as for theirs. A relationship with the Lord will improve any marriage.

> —*Dennis Newkirk*
> *Sr. Pastor,*
> *Henderson Hills Baptist Church*
> *Edmond, Oklahoma*

Never underestimate the impact of one kind word.

—Drs. Les and Leslie Parrott
Oklahoma Marriage Ambassadors

Marriage is the cornerstone of the most effective and important unit of government in our society—the family. And here in Oklahoma we have an opportunity to make our marriages all they were meant to be. We can build our marriages better and our state will be stronger for it.

—Steve Largent
Congressman
Tulsa, Oklahoma

Did You Know?

Healthy relationships can help us ward off depression, boost our immune systems, lower our cholesterol levels, increase our odds of surviving coronary disease, and keep stress hormones in check.

I'm not a real movie star. I've still got the same wife I started out with twenty-eight years ago.

—*Will Rogers*

First make a commitment to the Lord, then to each other.

> *—Melvin and Maggie Smith,*
> *married 1933*
> *Chandler, Oklahoma*

When they were teenagers, Melvin and Maggie worked in neighboring cotton fields. "The rows stopped at the fence," Maggie remembers with a grin, "so with a little timing, we could meet at the end of each row!" Melvin was a railway mail clerk for over thirty years; Maggie is a historian and author of twenty-four books.*

When you argue, keep to the subject. Too many times in anger it drifts into areas other than the problem.

—Larry and Kelly Patton,
married 1990
Lawton, Oklahoma

To love is to take delight in the happiness of another, or what amounts to the same, it is to account another's happiness one's own.

—*Gottfried Leibnitz*

Best Date Place in Oklahoma

At the top of the Bank of Oklahoma Building in downtown Tulsa. Everyone should have the chance to eat a wonderful meal from fifty-six stories high with the spouse that put you on top of the "world."

—Travis and Susan Meyer,
married 1985
Tulsa, Oklahoma

Oklahomans are known for their pioneering spirit. We have overcome the hardships of the dust bowl, famines, floods, tornadoes, and even a terrorist bombing that killed hundreds of our loved ones. But nothing defeats us—not even our alarming divorce rate. While it is an epidemic in our state, we will overcome it. Our pioneering spirit is what will help us reverse the divorce rate in our state.

—*Drs. Lori and Stewart Beasley*
Edmond, Oklahoma

Talk things out and never give up.

> —*Delbert and Wanda Wilkins,*
> *married 1943*
> *Lawton, Oklahoma*

Delbert and Wanda have had a busy life with eight children and a successful business. "You can talk and pray your way through most problems," says Wanda.

"And you don't have to *say* everything that you're *thinking*," Delbert adds with a laugh.*

To keep your marriage brimming, with love in the loving cup, whenever you're wrong, admit it, whenever you're right, shut up.

—*Ogden Nash*

There is a fly in the ointment of every good marriage. It's the disease-carrying insect of unmet expectations.

—Drs. Les and Leslie Parrott
Oklahoma Marriage Ambassadors

Relationships are ultimately a deep, mysterious, and unfathomable spiritual endeavor.

—Drs. Les and Leslie Parrott
Oklahoma Marriage Ambassadors

Advice to the wife:

Be to his virtues very kind.
Be to his faults a little blind.

—Anonymous

You should always remember why and what made you first fall in love with your spouse but continue to find new reasons to fall in love again and again.

—*Mike and Donna Jestes,*
married 1976

He who finds a wife finds what is good and receives favor from the LORD.

PROVERBS 18:22

My most brilliant achievement was to be able to persuade my wife to marry me.

—Winston Churchill

Resolve small conflicts promptly, before they become mountainous obstacles.

> —*Robert and Debbie Ahlborn,*
> *married 1969*
> *Owasso, Oklahoma*

Listen and keep an open mind about what your partner is saying, even if you don't want to hear it. Talk to each other about all things: little and big, important and unimportant.

> —*Judge Niles and Barbara Jackson,*
> *married 1975*
> *Oklahoma City, Oklahoma*

A happy marriage is a long conversation which always seems too short.

—*Andre Maurois*

Take the time to get to know your future partner. Marriage can be wonderfully fulfilling if you are working together as a team.

—Jennifer Eve Fish
Oklahoma City, Oklahoma

Faithfulness is like a multi-faceted jewel, exhibiting a complex combination of interrelated dimensions such as trust, commitment, truth, loyalty, valuing, and care.

> —Drs. Les and Leslie Parrott
> *Oklahoma Marriage Ambassadors*

Question to Ponder

It is said that men "report talk" and women "rapport talk." Do you find this to be true?

A successful marriage requires falling in love many times, always with the same person.

—*Mignon McLaughlin*

Two souls with but a single thought, two hearts that beat as one.

—Maria Lovell

Always be totally honest and open with each other.

—Paul and Georgia Bateman,
married 1942
Anadarko, Oklahoma

Paul and Georgia did a lot of talking before they were married and have never stopped. "Doesn't matter if it's big or small," says Georgia. "We talk over everything." When Paul returned from World War II (with four bronze stars), they bought a farm and began a small dairy.*

Love does not consist in gazing at each other but in looking in the same direction.

—Antoine DeSaint-Exupery

Commitment serves as a mooring when passion burns low and turbulent times and fierce impulses overtake us.

—Drs. Les and Leslie Parrott
Oklahoma Marriage Ambassadors

Most Romantic Place to Kiss in Oklahoma

At sunset at the top of Mt. Scott near Lawton because of the beauty and serenity.

> —*Timothy and Connie Sullivan,*
> *married 1971*
> *Tulsa, Oklahoma*

My husband just last Sunday in church took my hand and kissed it for no reason other than he loved and appreciated me.

> —*Lynden and Kathleen Wilcoxson,*
> *married 1982*
> *Oklahoma City, Oklahoma*

The difference between smooth sailing and shipwreck in marriage lies in what you as a couple are doing about the rough weather.

> —*Howard and Tracy Hendricks*
> *Director, Oklahoma Department*
> *of Human Services*
> *Oklahoma City, Oklahoma*

Life isn't always sunshine, learn to survive the storms.

—Guy and Mildred Harris,
married 1931
Nowata, Oklahoma

Guy and Mildred have lived on the same farm in northeast Oklahoma for over half a century. Guy stays active with chores and repairs; Mildred still cooks huge holiday meals for the family.*

Marriage Booster

- Make a list of the characteristics you like most about your spouse.
- You can present the list on a special occasion like a birthday or anniversary—or "just because."
- When you make a habit of accentuating the positive, love almost always grows faster and stronger for both the presenter and the receiver.

Wise up! The little things you do now—without thinking—will cut a life-long groove in your relationship.

—Drs. Les and Leslie Parrott
Oklahoma Marriage Ambassadors

Happy couples decide to be happy. In spite of the troubles life deals them, they make happiness a habit.

—Drs. Les and Leslie Parrott
Oklahoma Marriage Ambassadors

One of the most important things any of us can do is take a course or a seminar on relationships. We all need to continue learning new skills that will enhance and improve our relationships at home.

> —*Ernest L. Holloway*
> *President, Langston University*
> *Langston, Oklahoma*

Spend as much time together as possible.

> —Weslie and Marie Stabel, Sr.,
> married 1941
> Gage, Oklahoma

Weslie and Marie were introduced by Weslie's sister—a regular at the beauty shop where Marie worked. "We've had ups and downs like anyone else," says Marie, "but we always worked and prayed them through together." Wes owned a grade-A dairy for years and still maintains hay fields.*

Immature love says, "I love you because I need you."

Mature love says, "I need you because I love you."

—Erich Fromm

Best Date Place in Oklahoma

In a sailboat in the middle of Lake Hefner at sunset.

—Jim and Laura Cross, married 1976
Oklahoma City, Oklahoma

Roman Nose State Park

—Jay and Joan Swallow, married 1962
Geary, Oklahoma

Forgiveness in marriage can only heal when the focus is on what our spouses *do*, rather than who they *are*.

—Drs. Les and Leslie Parrott
Oklahoma Marriage Ambassadors

Instead of trying to make someone into the ideal partner, pour your energies into making yourself a better person.

—Drs. Les and Leslie Parrott
Oklahoma Marriage Ambassadors

Love is an act of endless forgiveness, a tender look which becomes a habit.

—*Peter Ustinov*

When faced with a mistake, forgive and go on.

—*Ollie and Hattie Sisk, married 1924*
Westville, Oklahoma

Ollie and Hattie went to school together in a one-room country schoolhouse. "We used to make music together," says Hattie. "Ollie had a guitar, and I played an old pump-organ." Hattie still remembers the moment Ollie sat her under a tree and said, "I want you to be my wife someday." She was thirteen at the time.*

The covenant of marriage is part of God's creative genius. It is one of the most important places we human beings learn about unconditional love, unconditional forgiveness, and unlimited grace. As we demonstrate these qualities in our homes we draw closer to God.

—Dr. Bruce Ewing
Pastor, Fellowship Bible Church
Tulsa, Oklahoma

Couples often think the grass is greener on the other side of the fence, only to find it has been painted.

—Rep. Jim Reese
Nardin, Oklahoma

Commitment creates a small island of certainty in the swirling waters of uncertainty.

—*Drs. Les and Leslie Parrott*
Oklahoma Marriage Ambassadors

The best marriages are made of moments when the simple joy of sharing life with the one you love transfuses all of life, even its painful difficulties, with a kind of haunting beauty. To fully appreciate them, though, you have to take the time. They can be neither rushed nor postponed.

—Richard Exley

A good marriage is a life-long partnership between a man and a woman. It requires love, planning, setting goals, managing, maintenance, cooperation, support, accountability, hard work, and periodic check-ups.

*—Homer and Vernice Lewis,
married 1954*

Questions to Ponder

When was the last time your spouse took priority over a project at work or an "important" deadline?

What we anticipate seldom occurs; what we least expect generally happens—especially in marriage!

—Drs. Les and Leslie Parrott
 Oklahoma Marriage Ambassadors

The habit of happiness is an inside job.

—Drs. Les and Leslie Parrott
Oklahoma Marriage Ambassadors

A marriage, like any other relationship, can be as good as both of the people involved are willing to make it.

—Leo and Susie Presley,
married 1978
Stillwater, Oklahoma

Successful couples take the raw materials of marriage—the good and bad they bring together as persons—and create their own unique and lasting bond.

—Drs. Les and Leslie Parrott
Oklahoma Marriage Ambassadors

Before criticizing your wife's faults, you must remember it may have been these very defects which prevented her from getting a better husband than the one she married.

—Anonymous

And the Lord God said, It is not good that the man should be alone; I will make him an help meet for him.

GENESIS 2:18 KJV

Therefore shall a man leave his father and his mother, and shall cleave unto his wife: and they shall be one flesh.

GENESIS 2:24 KJV

Marriages can never be perfect because people are never perfect!

> —Drs. Les and Leslie Parrott
> Oklahoma Marriage Ambassadors

Did You Know?

A major predictor of marital satisfaction is the husband's independence from his parents.

Bonding is the emotional covenant that links a man and woman together for life. It is the specialness which sets those two lovers apart from every other person on the face of the earth.

—*Desmond Morris*

Best Place to Kiss in Oklahoma

Falls Creek in the Arbuckles

—Ray and Jennifer Griffin,
married 1994
Broken Arrow, Oklahoma

The Tulsa pedestrian bridge across the Arkansas River—that's where my husband kneeled and proposed to me then waved at passing cars to announce our engagement. It's also a beautiful spot to cuddle and talk and watch an Oklahoma sunset.

—Jerry and Sue Dodd, married 1998
Tulsa, Oklahoma

In the measure that young passion recedes,

The vacancy is replaced with a deeper,
more abiding sense of intimacy,
care, and co-creativity.

As the flame fades,
deep-burning coals emerge.

—Drs. Les and Leslie Parrott
Oklahoma Marriage Ambassadors

No one can make another person unhappy. You can't often control your circumstances, but you can control your attitude toward those circumstances.

—*Drs. Les and Leslie Parrott*
Oklahoma Marriage Ambassadors

Work at becoming closer and closer.

*—Elmer and Emma Porter,
Oklahoma City, married 1921*

Emma first met Elmer while he was working in a friend's barbershop. "He seemed so nice and was nice-looking too!" she recalls. Elmer eventually owned his own barbershop, while Emma worked in a nearby grocery store. "We enjoyed just being together," says Emma.*

Best Date Place in Oklahoma

Walk together on a trail through the trees in any state park.

—C. Herman and Marieta Reece,
married 1953
Oklahoma City, Oklahoma

Sitting at a table in Utica Square in Tulsa on a warm summer evening, sharing a meal and watching the people.

—Dr. James and Ann Halligan,
married 1957
Stillwater, Oklahoma

No man or woman is a failure who has helped hold happily a home together. He who has been victorious in his home can never be completely defeated.

—*Robert W. Burns*

Resentment is to relationships as cancer is to the body. At first it is small and imperceptible, but over time it grows larger and spreads its poison throughout.

—Drs. Les and Leslie Parrott
Oklahoma Marriage Ambassadors

Commitment is not quite as difficult as it seems, but it does require a cool head and a steadfast heart.

—Drs. Les and Leslie Parrott
Oklahoma Marriage Ambassadors

To Maintain a . . .

Never brush off your wife's fears or hurt feelings as "silly."

Never stop romancing your spouse.

Never keep a running list of your husband's mistakes and shortcomings.

... Happy Marriage

Always assure your wife that you are there for her no matter what.

Always make sure you and your spouse have time alone together.

Always forgive and encourage.

You can never be happily married to another until you get a divorce from yourself. Successful marriage demands a certain death to self.

—Jerry McCant

When the scales of a relationship are unbalanced—one person is always giving and one is always receiving—both will eventually feel cheated.

—Drs. Les and Leslie Parrott
Oklahoma Marriage Ambassadors

Don't fuss about every little thing. Work on being agreeable.

—Cecil and Nola Critchfield,
married 1926
Chandler, Oklahoma

Cecil and Nola first met as children but weren't married until in their twenties. Cecil spent most of his life working for telephone and electric companies. "We never had much," says Nola, "but we always had each other!"*

The deepest kind of sharing can take place only when there is no fear of rejection.

—Les and Leslie Parrott
Oklahoma Marriage Ambassadors

Live so that you wouldn't be ashamed to sell the family parrot to the town gossip.

—*Will Rogers*

Marriage means giving up a carefree lifestyle and coming to terms with new limits. It means unexpected inconveniences!

—Drs. Les and Leslie Parrott
Oklahoma Marriage Ambassadors

The Governor and First Lady's Marriage Initiative is not only groundbreaking for our state and our country, it just may be one of the most important things that has ever happened in Oklahoma. When Governor Keating announced his vision for reducing the Oklahoma divorce rate by a third in the next decade, I realized our state has an opportunity to become a beacon for our nation in one of the single most important social causes of our day.

—Mike Hunter
Oklahoma Secretary of State
Oklahoma City, Oklahoma

Love is giving more and never keeping score.

—David Ingles

Compliments feel good—both to give and to receive.

—Drs. Les and Leslie Parrott
Oklahoma Marriage Ambassadors

Love must be learned, and learned, again and again: there is no end to it.

—*Katherine Anne Porter*

A good marriage is built by two people's capacity to adjust to bad things.

—*Drs. Les and Leslie Parrott*
  Oklahoma Marriage Ambassadors

Romeo and Juliet, Lancelot and Guinevere, Rhett and Scarlett, even Jack and Rose from the cinematic tale of the Titanic—each snuffed out their powerful love while the heat of passion was turned up full blast. Why? Because it couldn't last. The heat of passion was never meant to. Can you imagine Romeo and Juliet grocery shopping?

—Drs. Les and Leslie Parrott
Oklahoma Marriage Ambassadors

Conclusion

Since you have taken the time to thumb through this little book, I know you are interested in marriage. More than that, I know you are interested in building better marriages in Oklahoma. And that says a lot about your values and your character. I want to commend you for that and invite you to stand with thousands of other people across our great state who are concerned about our skyrocketing divorce rate. More than that, I want to urge you to do what you can to help couples in your own community get married well and stay happily married for life. How can you do this? Perhaps you could be a mentor to a newlywed couple. Perhaps you could encourage a couple in need to seek professional help. Perhaps you could recommend a good marriage book to a couple who might need it. Or perhaps the best thing you could do is to be sure your marriage is rock solid. Whatever it is that you might do to help our great State of Oklahoma build better marriages, I want to thank you on behalf of Governor and First Lady Keating, as well our Marriage Ambassadors, Drs. Les and Leslie Parrott. It is because of people like you we are all proud to be Oklahomans.

Jerry Regier
Secretary of Health and Human Services
Oklahoma City, Oklahoma

About the Authors

Drs. Les and Leslie Parrott are co-directors of the Center for Relationships Development at Seattle Pacific University (SPU), a groundbreaking program dedicated to teaching the basics of good relationships. Les Parrott is a professor of clinical psychology at SPU, and Leslie is a marriage and family therapist at SPU. The Parrotts are authors of the Gold Medallion Award-winning *Saving Your Marriage Before It Starts, Becoming Soul Mates, Love Is,* and *When Bad Things Happen To Good Marriages.* They have been featured on *Oprah, CBS This Morning, CNN,* and *The View,* and in *USA Today* and the *New York Times.* They are also frequent guest speakers and have written for a variety of magazines. The Parrotts serve as marriage ambassadors and scholars in residence for the Oklahoma Governor's Marriage Initiative. Visit www.RealRelationships.com to learn more about Les and Leslie's speaking schedule and their resources.

Additional copies of this book and other titles by
Les and Leslie Parrott are available from your local bookstore
and at <www.RealRelationship.com>.

If you have enjoyed this book, or if it has impacted your life,
we would like to hear from you.

Please contact us at:
RiverOak Publishing
Department E
P.O. Box 700143
Tulsa, Oklahoma 74170-0143

Visit our website at:
www.RiverOakPublishing.com